Plant Reproduction

How Do You Grow a GIANT Pumpkin?

Cath Senker

raintree
a Capstone company — publishers for children

Raintree is an imprint of Capstone Global Library Limited, a company incorporated in England and Wales having its registered office at 7 Pilgrim Street, London, EC4V 6LB – Registered company number: 6695582

www.raintreepublishers.co.uk
myorders@raintreepublishers.co.uk

Text © Capstone Global Library Limited 2014
First published in hardback in 2014
Paperback edition first published in 2015
The moral rights of the proprietor have been asserted.

All rights reserved. No part of this publication may be reproduced in any form or by any means (including photocopying or storing it in any medium by electronic means and whether or not transiently or incidentally to some other use of this publication) without the written permission of the copyright owner, except in accordance with the provisions of the Copyright, Designs and Patents Act 1988 or under the terms of a licence issued by the Copyright Licensing Agency, Saffron House, 6–10 Kirby Street, London EC1N 8TS (www.cla.co.uk). Applications for the copyright owner's written permission should be addressed to the publisher.

Edited by Adam Miller, Sian Smith, and Penny West
Designed by Philippa Jenkins
Picture research by Tracy Cummins
Originated by Capstone Global Library Ltd
Produced by Victoria Fitzgerald
Printed and bound in China by CTPS

ISBN 978 1 406 27429 5 (hardback)
17 16 15 14 13
10 9 8 7 6 5 4 3 2 1

ISBN 978 1 406 27436 3 (paperback)
18 17 16 15 14
10 9 8 7 6 5 4 3 2 1

Senker, Cath
Plant Reproduction: How Do You Grow a Giant Pumpkin? (Show Me Science)
A full catalogue record for this book is available from the British Library.

Acknowledgements
We would like to thank the following for permission to reproduce photographs:
Alamy pp. 18 (© John Swithinbank), 21 (© John Robertson), 23 (© Mark Sadlier); Corbis pp. 15 right (© Ocean), 28 (© Ocean), 29 (© Angela Coppola/weestock); Getty Images pp. 8 (Aaron Foster), 11 (Christopher Furlong), 12 (Don Nichols), 19 (Daly and Newton), 22 (Ottmar Diez), 24 (Justin Sullivan), 25 (Marco Secchi), 26 (Christopher Furlong), 27 (BERND WEISSBROD/AFP); Photo Researchers pp. 14 (Nigel Cattlin / Science Source), 20 (Picture Partners); Photoshot p. 7 top (Photos Horticultural/Michael Warren); Shutterstock pp. 4, 7 bottom (© Tischenko Irina), 9 (© cowboy54), 10 (© saiko3p), 13 (© Sayanjo65), 15 left (© ER_09), 16 (© vita khorzhevska), 17 (© Mike Golay).

Cover photograph of a miniature pumpkin on top of a giant pumpkin at the 34th Annual Safeway World Championship Pumpkin Weigh-Off, October 8, 2007 in Half Moon Bay, California, USA reproduced with permission of Getty Images (Justin Sullivan).

We would like to thank Ann Fullick for her invaluable help in the preparation of this book.
Every effort has been made to contact copyright holders of material reproduced in this book. Any omissions will be rectified in subsequent printings if notice is given to the publishers.

Disclaimer
All the Internet addresses (URLs) given in this book were valid at the time of going to press. However, due to the dynamic nature of the Internet, some addresses may have changed, or sites may have changed or ceased to exist since publication. While the author and publishers regret any inconvenience this may cause readers, no responsibility for any such changes can be accepted by either the author or the publishers.

Contents

Fruit or vegetable? 4
Plant parts 6
Seeds and bulbs 8
How do seeds grow? 10
Caring for seedlings 12
Bursting into bloom 14
Pollinate your pumpkin 16
Going for the biggest 18
Growing for success 20
Pests and problems 22
The giant vegetable contest 24
What can you do with giant vegetables? 26
Grow your own! 28
Glossary 30
Find out more 31
Index 32

Some words are shown in bold, **like this**. You can find out what they mean by looking in the glossary.

Fruit or vegetable?

Have you heard of the story of Jack and the giant beanstalk? Perhaps you thought it was just a fairy story. But giant vegetables are real! Learning about growing giant vegetables for contests can show us how plants grow and **reproduce**.

Vegetables

What is the difference between fruits and vegetables? When we cook, we think of vegetables as savoury foods, such as tomatoes and runner beans. But scientists say that a vegetable is a part of a plant you can eat, though not the part with seeds in it. Any vegetable that contains seeds is a fruit. Many plants we call vegetables are actually fruits, such as pumpkins, tomatoes, and cucumbers.

Have you tried all of these vegetables?

Fruits

When we cook, we think of fruits as sweet foods. You make rhubarb crumble with rhubarb, so it is a fruit. But rhubarb comes from the stem of the plant, so in fact it is a vegetable.

Now you know the difference between fruits and vegetables, come on a giant fruit-and vegetable-growing journey, from sowing seeds and caring for plants to harvesting enormous foods. Watch out for the giant pumpkin!

Vegetables that are actually fruits

- avocado
- beans, such as runner beans
- cucumber
- pepper
- pumpkin
- tomato

Max and the giant pumpkin

Max, age six, from Yorkshire, UK, and his older brother and sister held a pumpkin-growing competition. Max was determined to win. He watered his pumpkin regularly. At night, he kept it warm with a blanket. Max's pumpkin grew into a 92-kilogram (203-pound) monster – the largest of the three and the clear winner. It weighed four times as much as Max!

Plant parts

Have you noticed the different parts of plants? Three important parts are the leaves, stem, and roots. Each has a special job to help the plant to grow.

Leaves make food for the plant. To do this, they use light from the Sun, a gas called carbon dioxide from the air, and water. This process is called **photosynthesis**. During photosynthesis, leaves give off oxygen from tiny openings.

The stem keeps the plant up straight so that the leaves are in sunlight. It carries the water and **nutrients** to the different parts of the plant.

Roots hold the plant in the soil. They take up water and nutrients from the soil. Nutrients are substances that help the plant to grow well. In the same way, we need vitamins to make us healthy.

leaves

stem

seed

roots

A walking stick from a cabbage

Giant fruits and vegetables have enormous plant parts. The giant walking stick cabbage has a tall, straight, and hard stem. When the cabbage is ripe, you cut off the vegetable and roots. You hang the stem up to dry until it is as solid as a baseball bat. Then you can use it as a walking stick!

HOW PLANTS HELP US

Plants give us food. Also, the oxygen they release forms a vital part of the air we breathe.

Seeds and bulbs

Many new plants start off from seeds or bulbs. A seed is a tiny container with everything that is needed to make a new plant. A bulb is a plant part that grows under the ground. It is a winter food store for the plant and can also grow into a new plant.

The wind blows away the dandelion seeds.

Birds eat the seeds of many plants.

Seed send-off

Plants produce many seeds. But they do not want the seeds to grow right next to them, because the new plants will compete for space and water. So they **disperse** them.

Plants send off their seeds in different ways. Some seeds are blown away by the wind. Others are eaten by animals – often birds. The birds fly away and later the seeds come out in their droppings (poo). Many seeds end up in places where they cannot grow, but some become new plants.

Giant genes

To grow giant vegetables or fruits, you need special seeds or bulbs that come from giant **varieties**. They have **genes** to make them grow big. Genes are the instructions inside the **cells** of a living thing for how it will look, such as its size and colour.

Top-price seed

Some giant pumpkin growers are so keen to find top seeds that they will pay an enormous price. In 2010, Chris Stevens from New Richmond, Wisconsin, USA, grew a giant pumpkin that weighed 821 kilograms (1,810 pounds). He sold a single seed from it for £1,000 ($1,600)!

How do seeds grow?

Seeds rest in the ground until the time is right to grow. Most wait until spring, when the days become warmer and the hours of daylight longer.

Germination

When seeds start to grow, it is called **germination**. Seeds need water, air, and warmth to germinate. First, the seed takes in water from the soil. The baby root bursts through the seed and grows downwards. Then the shoot pops out and grows upwards.

Giant vegetable seeds start off just the same way. In April or May, sow your giant pumpkin seeds in plant pots 15 centimetres (6 inches) tall. To give them a head start, sow them with lots of compost. Compost is made from dead plants that have rotted. They form a rich soil full of **nutrients**.

Compost helps these pumpkin **seedlings** to grow big and strong.

To speed up germination, place your seeds in a warm place, such as over a hot water tank. But do not put them too close to the heat or they will die.

Know your onions

In 2012, Peter Glazebrook, from Newark in Nottinghamshire, UK, grew the world's heaviest onion. It was a massive 8 kilograms (18 pounds) – the weight of around 50 normal onions! He planted the seeds in October and did not harvest his crop until the following September. If you want to beat Peter's record, you will need lots of patience. It has taken him 25 years to perfect his growing method!

Caring for seedlings

Once they have **germinated**, **seedlings** need water, light, and warmth to grow well. Nature provides all of these, but growers can help out.

The plant takes in water through its roots. Tiny root hairs take in water and pass it on to the small roots. It then travels into the main roots and up the stem to the leaves.

Watering

Growers water their plants, but are careful not to over-water. Did you know that more plants are killed by over-watering them than by not watering them enough? The tiny root hairs need oxygen. If the soil around them is too wet, they cannot get enough oxygen to do their job properly.

- main root
- small roots
- tiny root hairs

Cosy pumpkins

You know how a tent keeps you warm at night when you are camping? Some growers provide clear plastic tents for each pumpkin seedling. Inside each tent is a special light bulb that is switched on during cold nights. These light bulbs give out lots of heat as well as light. The seedlings grow quickly.

Warmth and light

The Sun provides warmth and light. Many growers keep seedlings warmer in a greenhouse. The glass or plastic allows light to enter, but protects the plants from the wind and chilly spring nights. Some keen gardeners place lights in the greenhouse so their plants enjoy a longer growing day.

These are tomato seedlings, 20 days after sowing.

Bursting into bloom

When the **seedlings** have grown into full-sized plants, flower **buds** appear. These open up into flowers. Flowers are important for plant reproduction.

Flowers and reproduction

Most flowers have both male and female parts. The **stamen** is the male part of the flower, which makes **pollen**. It is made up of the **anther** and **filament**. The anther contains pollen and the filament holds up the anther.

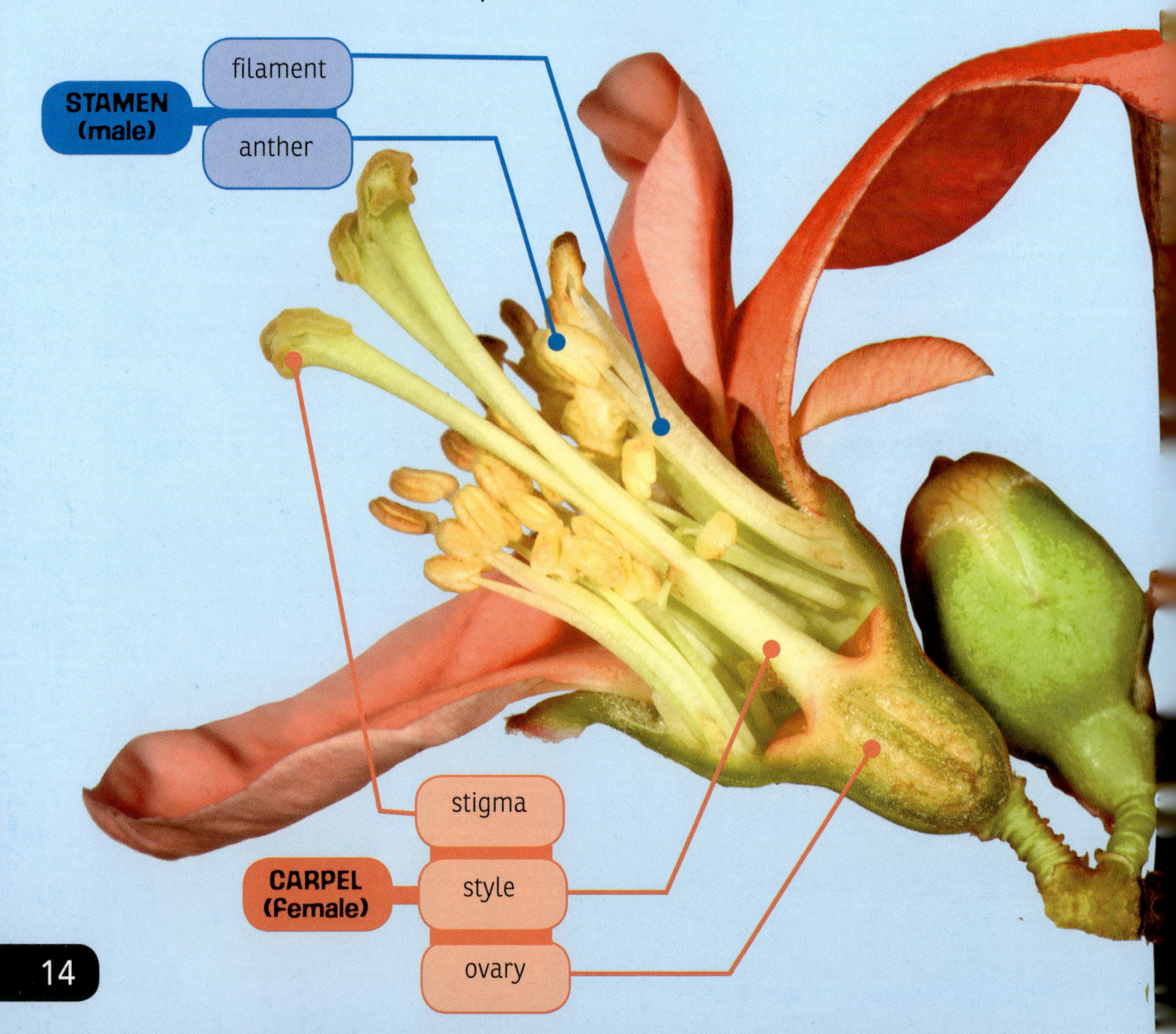

STAMEN (male)
- filament
- anther

CARPEL (Female)
- stigma
- style
- ovary

The female pumpkin flower has an ovary below, which will become the fruit.

ovary

female pumpkin flower

male pumpkin flower

The **carpel** is the female part of the flower, where seeds are made. It has the **stigma**, the **style**, and the **ovary**. The stigma is sticky so that pollen grains will stick to it. The style holds up the stigma. At the bottom of the style is the ovary, which contains the **ovules** – the eggs.

Giant pumpkins produce separate male and female flowers. The male flowers arrive first. Then the female flowers bloom.

Non-flowering plants

Some plants, such as ferns and mosses, do not produce flowers and seeds. Instead they make spores – tiny pieces of living material. The spores can grow into new plants.

FLOWERS GOOD ENOUGH TO EAT

Did you know that cauliflowers and broccoli are the buds of flowers? So you have probably eaten flowers for dinner. You can sprinkle pretty orange marigold and nasturtium flowers on salads, too. Rose petals add a strong flavour to desserts.

Pollinate your pumpkin

The next step is **pollination**. The word "pollination" comes from **pollen** – a yellow, dust-like substance. For pollination to happen, pollen has to move from the **stamen** (male part) of one flower to the **carpel** (female part) of another flower.

Wind-blown pollen

Some plants rely on the wind to blow the pollen from flower to flower. Many trees, shrubs, and grasses make small, light pollen that is easily carried in the wind.

Insect pollination

Other plants produce bright, attractive flowers with sweet scents. They attract insects, such as bees and butterflies. The insects fly down into the flower to find the tasty **nectar** at the base of the petals. On the way, their bodies brush past the **anther** and **stigma**. They pick up pollen from the anther, and pollen rubs off onto the sticky stigma.

The wind blows the pollen from this grass.

A bee pollinates a pumpkin flower.

When pollen on the stigma joins with an **ovule** (egg), a seed is made. This is called **fertilization**. The flower has done its job, so it dies. The **ovary** remains, and it forms a fruit to protect the seeds growing inside.

A HELPING HAND

Giant pumpkin growers hand pollinate their pumpkins to make sure fertilization happens. Also, the quicker the pumpkins are pollinated, the more time they will have to grow huge. Growers rub the pollen from the anthers on the male flowers onto the stigmas of the female ones.

Going for the biggest

If you want to produce truly enormous fruits, you have to select which fruits to keep. The more fruits a plant has, the smaller they will be. They all compete for water and **nutrients**.

A grower prunes pumpkin stems.

A tight fit

Giant cucumbers grow so large they need to be supported. This prevents them breaking under their own weight. Some growers place the cucumbers in the legs of pairs of tights, tied to a support at the top. The world's longest cucumber was grown by Clare Pearce in the UK in 2010. It measured 119 centimetres (47 inches) – about four times the length of a normal cucumber.

Growers choose a few of the fastest-growing fruits to keep. They prune (cut off) the smaller ones. They also cut off the rest of the flowers, so no more fruits develop. But they keep all the leaves, because they produce food for the plant.

A few weeks later, growers decide on the best-growing single fruit to keep. Then it will receive all the nutrients and grow large.

Don't get squashed!

In 2011, Joel Jarvis from Ontario, Canada, grew a prize-winning squash that weighed more than 670 kilograms (1,477 pounds). That is as heavy as a polar bear! In its peak growing phase, it gained 18 kilograms (40 pounds) every day – the weight of a five-year-old child.

Growing for success

So how you can you grow the perfect giant vegetable or fruit? Vegetables in the supermarket are normally all similar shapes and sizes. The supermarkets have selected the best ones. But in nature, vegetables vary a lot. What can you do to ensure success?

Carrots can grow in strange shapes!

Shape

The shape of a vegetable depends on how it grows. A carrot is a root vegetable that grows downwards in the soil. If the growing tip meets a stone, it will grow to the side to avoid it. The carrot will not turn out perfectly straight.

Some gardeners train their vegetables to grow to a certain shape. One gardener grows parsnips in pipes attached to the side of a barn. They grow downwards to form incredibly long, thin shapes.

Talking to your vegetables

Clive Bevan from Northamptonshire, UK, grows enormous pumpkins. He thinks that talking to the plants helps them to grow. Could there be any truth in this? When we speak, our breath gives out carbon dioxide. Plants use carbon dioxide in **photosynthesis**. But scientists have found no evidence that talking to plants really does help growth.

Clive Bevan at his allotment with a pumpkin he hopes will become a giant.

Size

Growers have several methods for producing super-sized vegetables. Chinese farmer Akele Hi grows massive cucumbers. His secret is shovelling horse dung (poo) onto the plants as **fertilizer**. Fertilizers are **nutrients** that help plants grow faster and bigger.

FLYING PUMPKINS

Some of Clive Bevan's pumpkins have weighed more than 140 kilograms (over 300 pounds) – so heavy he needed a helicopter to lift them!

Pests and problems

Watch out! Pests such as slugs, snails, and various insects can munch your fruits and vegetables. Diseases may also damage plants. If the leaves, stems, or roots are damaged, it becomes hard for plants to make food and draw up water.

Pest prevention

Some gardeners use chemical sprays to kill the pests or diseases. But these may kill helpful insects, too, such as bees and ladybirds.

Slugs can destroy crops, such as these lettuces.

The incredible exploding pumpkin

Steve Connolly from Sharon, Massachusetts, USA grew five splendid giant pumpkins. But one by one, four of his prized vegetables exploded. How could this happen? Giant pumpkins normally gain 18 kilograms (40 pounds) a day. If it rains a lot, they may grow by 22 kilograms (49 pounds) daily. The pumpkin expands too quickly, putting pressure on the skin. The effect is like blowing up a balloon too much. The weaker parts of the skin cannot stand the pressure, and the pumpkin bursts.

Others use **organic** (natural) methods to deal with pests. They use natural chemicals that do not harm other wildlife, such as soap sprays. They may cover plants with fine netting to stop pests from reaching them. Another way is to grow plants nearby that pests hate, such as garlic. Natural **predators** are useful, too – creatures that eat the pests. Frogs and toads eat slugs and snails, as do many birds.

Sunscreen

Plants need sunlight, but too much heat can make the leaves wither and die. Some growers shade their giant vegetables with tents or large umbrellas.

The giant vegetable contest

Finally, the giant vegetables are fully grown. It is competition time! Often growers have to store their precious vegetables overnight in a room at the competition site. Green vegetables suffer because they contain lots of water. For example, a green cabbage is 93 per cent water. The cabbage loses water from its leaves through **evaporation** and the leaves go limp. Pumpkins are 90 per cent water. But the water is trapped inside the thick skin, so it does not evaporate as quickly.

Giant pumpkins are on display at this contest.

The contest

On the big day, competition vegetables must look perfect, with no damage. Growers make sure they look clean and neat.

The judges examine the vegetables carefully. They weigh giant fruits and vegetables, such as cabbages, pumpkins, marrows, and tomatoes. Long, thin vegetables, such as runner beans and cucumbers, are measured. The judges announce the winners in the different classes, such as "heaviest marrow" or "longest runner bean". The victorious growers collect their prizes.

Competition cheat

In 2011, Barry Truss from Shropshire, UK was caught cheating to make his giant pumpkin weigh an incredible 84 kilograms (186 pounds). He had filled the pumpkin with water and plugged up the hole. Truss was found out after someone overheard him telling a friend. The judges at Beckbury Allotment Association said Truss would be allowed to compete again, but they would use special equipment to check his pumpkins.

What can you do with giant vegetables?

After the contest, many growers share their **produce** out among friends and family. The world's largest squash, weighing 670 kilograms (1,477 pounds), would make soup for more than 5,000 people!

Giant fruits and vegetables can be just as tasty to eat as normal ones. But some grow so massive they taste disgusting. For example, when giant pumpkins develop beyond their natural size, the flesh can become tough. They have taken in so much water that they lose their flavour.

Jonathan Walker lifts the heaviest marrow in 2012.

A pumpkin-boat racer paddles in Germany.

So what else can you do with them? Weightlifter Jonathan Walker uses them for weight training. At a UK show in 2012, he lifted a prize-winning marrow, weighing 54 kilograms (120 pounds), above his head.

Pumpkin-boat racing

In many places in the United States, there is an annual pumpkin-boat race. Competitors hollow out the flesh of the pumpkins to make their boats. The tough skin is waterproof. Most people use paddles to push their pumpkins through the water. Some keen racers attach motors to their pumpkins to make them go faster.

World Championship Punkin' Chunkin'

"Punkin' chunkin'" is the sport of flinging pumpkins. At the event, competitors use different devices, such as slingshots, catapults, and trebuchets (giant catapults), to fling their pumpkins as far as they can. The pumpkins have to remain whole after leaving the devices. As of 2013, the world-record punkin' chunk was 1,367 metres (4,485 feet)!

Grow your own!

Why not try growing your own giant fruits and vegetables? The **produce** you buy in supermarkets has often been grown far away and then transported. It can be several days old when it reaches you. It may have been sprayed with chemicals to make it grow better.

Growers plant seeds in a vegetable garden.

Size is not everything

At the Ready Steady Pumpkin competition in New Zealand in 2012, children could enter their pumpkin in three categories: biggest, ugliest, or best dressed!

Farmers often grow **varieties** that can last a long time and are easy to transport. At home, you can grow varieties with the best taste. You can pick and eat them on the same day.

Growing tips

Here is how to grow your own giant pumpkin or other monster produce at home or school:

- plant your seeds in fresh compost in pots
- carefully move your **seedlings** once the first true leaves have grown (not the very first baby leaves)
- find a luxury home for your seedlings in a sunny spot of **fertilized** soil with plenty of space. Giant pumpkins need a patch about 50 square metres (500 square feet) to grow in
- when your plants flower, **pollinate** them
- select the healthiest, fastest-growing fruits and give them five-star care. Use the information in this book and the books and websites listed on page 31 to help you. Good luck!

Glossary

anther top part of the male part of a flower that makes pollen

bud swelling on a plant stem with tiny parts of a flower, ready to bloom into a flower, leaf, or stem

carpel female parts of a flower that contain the ovules (eggs)

cell tiny unit that all living things are made out of

disperse move away in different directions

evaporation process of a liquid changing into a gas. For example, when leaves become hot, the water inside them evaporates into the air.

fertilization moment when a male sex cell joins with a female egg, to start a new life

fertilizer substance added to soil to make plants grow better

filament part of a flower that holds up the anther

genes sections of DNA that control an inherited feature

germinate, germination when a seed starts to grow

nectar sugary substance that plants make to attract insects

nutrient substance that is taken in by an animal or plant to help it grow

organic without human-made chemicals

ovary female sex cell that becomes a fruit with seeds inside

ovule egg that becomes a seed after fertilization

photosynthesis process where plants make their own food using water, a gas called carbon dioxide in the air, and energy from sunlight

pollen special dust made by plants that contains the male sex cells

pollinate, pollination when pollen is carried from the anthers of one flower to the stigma of another one

predator animal that kills and eats other animals

produce fruits or vegetables grown by a gardener or farmer

reproduce when a living thing produces young like itself

seedling young plant that has grown from a seed

stamen male part of a flower that makes pollen

stigma female part of a flower that receives pollen

style stalk that holds up the stigma of a flower

variety several different sorts of the same thing

Find out more

Books
Europe's Most Amazing Plants (Plant Top Tens), Angela Royston and Michael Scott (Raintree, 2009)

Good Growing: A Kid's Guide to Green Gardening (Klutz, 2011)

Plants (Super Science), Richard Robinson (QED Publishing, 2008)

Vicious Veg (Horrible Science), Nick Arnold (Scholastic, 2008)

Websites
www.bbc.co.uk/bitesize/ks2/science/living_things/help_plants_grow/read/3
This website explains what different parts of plants do.

www.bbc.co.uk/bitesize/ks2/science/living_things/plants/play
There is a game about plant growth on this website.

www.mikecurtis.org.uk/ks2_plant_reproduction.htm
You can learn about reproduction in flowering plants here.

www.rhs.org.uk/children/for-kids
The Royal Horticultural Society's website has pages about plants for children.

DVDs
The Private Life of Plants, David Attenborough (2entertain, 2012)

Places to visit
Eden Project
Bodelva
St Austell
Cornwall
PL24 2SG
www.edenproject.com

RHS Garden Wisley
Woking
Surrey
GU23 6QB
www.rhs.org.uk/gardens/wisley

Index

anthers 14, 16, 17
avocados 5

broccoli 15
buds 14, 15
bulbs 8

cabbages 7, 24, 25
carbon dioxide 6, 21
carpels 14, 15, 16
carrots 20
cauliflowers 15
cells 9
chemical sprays 22
competitions 5, 24–25, 29
compost 10, 29
cucumbers 4, 5, 19, 21, 25

diseases 22

evaporation 24

ferns and mosses 15
fertilization 17
fertilizers 21, 29
filaments 14
flavour 26
flowers 14–15, 16, 17, 19
fruits 17, 18, 19
fruits and vegetables, differences between 4–5

genes 9
germination 10, 11
giant fruits and vegetables 7, 9, 10, 11, 19, 21, 23, 24–27

greenhouses 13
growing your own 28–29

hand pollination 17

insect pollination 16

leaves 6, 19

marrows 25, 26, 27

nectar 16
netting 23
nutrients 6, 10, 18, 21

onions 11
organic pest control 23
ovaries 14, 15, 17
ovules 15, 17
oxygen 6, 7, 12

parsnips 20
peppers 5
pests 22–23
photosynthesis 6, 21
plant parts 6–7
plant supports 19
pollen 14, 15, 16, 17
pollination 16–17, 29
predators, natural 23
pruning 18, 19
pumpkin-boat race 27
pumpkins 4, 5, 9, 10, 13, 15, 17, 21, 23, 24, 25, 26, 29
punkin' chunkin' sport 27

rhubarb 5
root hairs 12
roots 6, 10, 12
runner beans 5, 25

seed dispersal 8, 9
seedlings 10, 12–13, 14, 29
seeds 4, 8, 9, 10–11, 28, 29
shade 23
shapes, vegetable 20
shoots 10
slugs and snails 22, 23
soap sprays 23
spores 15
squashes 19, 26
stamens 14, 16
stems 6
stigmas 15, 16, 17
styles 14, 15
sunlight 13, 23

talking to plants 21
tomatoes 4, 5, 13, 25

uses for giant fruits and vegetables 26–27

varieties 9, 29

warmth 11, 13
water 6, 10, 12, 18, 24, 25, 26
watering 12
wind-blown pollen 16